THE COMPLETE
ILLUSTRATED AND ANNOTATED
UNDERWATER GLOSSARY

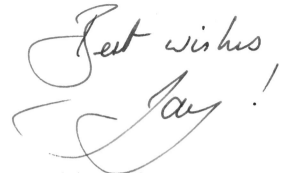

Best wishes
Jay!

THE COMPLETE
ILLUSTRATED AND ANNOTATED
UNDERWATER GLOSSARY

BY

Jay

The Complete Illustrated and Annotated Underwater Glossary is published by
Submex, 19 Roland Way, London SW7 3RF.   e-mail: submex@submex.co.uk

COPYRIGHT © 2005, Submex.

British Library Cataloguing in Publication Data.
A catalogue record for this book is available from the British Library.

ISBN: 0 9508242 4 0

Design: Ann Bevan.
Printed and bound in Scotland by Highland Printers Limited.

CONTENTS

Jay is the resident cartoonist at *Underwater Contractor International,* a bi-monthly magazine published by

Underwater World Publications Ltd, 55 High Street, Teddington, Middlesex, TW11 8HA
www.under-water.co.uk   E-mail: enquiries@divermag.co.uk

INTRODUCTION

In the beginning, when I was still wet behind the ears, I was reluctant to ask my peers what some technical term meant. I was afraid of revealing my own ignorance. I struggled on for years totally clueless.

Eventually I decided to educate myself. No longer would I nod knowingly at incomprehensible comments. It was time to learn. So I turned into a worm of the book kind. I became a worm that turned.

I went on a quest for the holy grail of enlightenment. The culmination of this daring expedition is what you see before you. This priceless treasure, this font of knowledge, this jewel of literature, this inestimably valuable recycled tree, I now share with you. Global underwater expertise takes a quantum leap forward with this ground-breaking, trend-setting, challenging and controversial publication.

And they said it would never be printed.

But 'reckless' is my middle name.

TYPES OF DIVER

Divers can be divided into distinctly diverse divisions. To elucidate, I hereby divulge the definitive digest on the diversity of divers, without diverting, diverging or deviating.

Ancient civilisation divers

Mystery still surrounds this earliest type of diver. Some authorities claim that they were aliens from another planet. These extra-terrestrials visited earth and introduced their advanced technologies to mankind when humans were still preoccupied with the proper way to eat a banana. Fortunately, since that time diving has advanced significantly. There is still some dispute about the etiquette of eating bananas.

Asyrian diver I

A bas-relief in the British Museum appears to depict the first recorded use of divers by the Assyrians, way back in 900BC. They haven't been seen since. They may still be down there!

"Assyrians? They went that way."

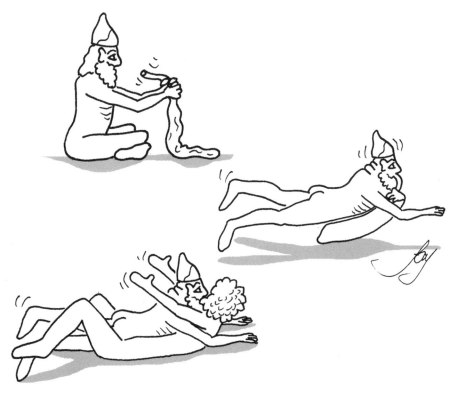

Assyrian diver 2

The amazing discovery of two more bas-reliefs at the British Museum has cast doubt on the Assyrian Diver Theory.

Baby diver

New young divers are desperately needed in the industry to defuse the 'personnel time bomb'. These so-called 'baby divers' require the guidance and close supervision of their more experienced colleagues. We should, therefore, adopt a patient and paternal attitude to the new influx.

Bounce diver

By definition, the bounce diver does not stay down for very long before he returns. The most daring bounce divers have the longest umbilicals.

Burglar diver

Sadly, occasionally a diver falls foul of the law. This is an occupational hazard of working in an environment where the hapless diver is surrounded by infinite quantities of temptingly desirable materials.

"Are you going to tell him it's a sea urchin,
or shall I?"

Clearance diver 1

One of the many tasks of the Royal Navy
Clearance Diver is to render marine mines safe.
The dangerous task requires intensive training.
Recognition of many different devices forms an
important part of the training regime.

Clearance diver 2

These fearless and highly trained military divers can defuse a mine with their eyes closed. They can tell instantly whether or not a mine is dangerous. Their motto is, "If it is ticking it is still OK".

"I give in diver. What's round and ticks?"

"Dammit. Another three floating voters."

Committee diver

Some divers specialise in being on committees, Unfortunately, some are not natural decision-makers.

Diver selection

Selecting the right type of diver for a particular job is an important factor in diving operations management. Different divers have different skills and abilities. Choosing the wrong diver can render the job impossible to do.

Ivor wondered if he was the right diver for the job.

"Congratulations Ivor. Don't forget, from now on the answer to every question will be 'because I'm the supervisor'."

Diving supervisor 1

Part of the training to become a diving supervisor is learning a vast amount of diving theory. This is so that the diving supervisor can confidently answer any question about diving.

Diving supervisor 2

Not every diver can become a supervisor.
It takes a special type of personality.
The diving supervisor must be a good leader and
have a natural air of authority. These skills can be
acquired with special training.

"He's never been the same since the
supervisor course."

"Well, at least it's quicker than the tube."

Exhibition diver

Exhibition divers never miss the opportunity to visit underwater exhibitions. Popular events attract divers from all over the world. Special arrangements are often necessary to cater for the large numbers of visitors. Queues are likely.

Fish farm diver

Fish farm divers, though growing in number, are not well-known in the diving industry. These shy, reclusive divers limit their activities to secluded coastal locations in remote parts of the world. Readers will be able to identify this elusive diver from this illustration, sketched during an actual sighting.

Frogman

With his rubber suit and flippers the frogman is easily distinguishable from the modern commercial diver. This adventurous diver, though abundant in the early 20th century, is rarely referred to as such today. The 'frogman' has now metamorphosed into the 'scoobedoo'.

"You don't have to be afraid of a frogman", said Ivor, re-assuring his son.

Great Northern diver

Also known as the Common Loon, the
Great Northern diver is rarely seen
nowadays. Solitary by habit, it can be
found in northern parts of the country
and occasionally in inland waters. Great
Northern divers are easily distinguishable
from other divers – they have bigger and
heavier heads and, on land, they are heavy-
footed, clumsy and barely able to walk.
Here is a glimpse of one in its natural
habitat.

Greek sponge diver

The dare-devil stunts of the Greek sponge diver are famed throughout the world. These fearless divers are descended (rapidly) from Ancient Greeks. Legend has it that a group of them once hid inside a Trojan sea-horse to avoid a Greek diver bearing gifts.

High diver

High divers flowered in the 1960s and are remarkable in that many claim not to inhale. Despite thermal protection they frequently declare that they are chilled out or cool. High divers are remarkably relaxed under pressure and want to be every diver's best buddy. The illustration captures the grace and skill of the high diver inaction.

Inland/inshore diver

Unlike the more fortunate offshore diver, the inland diver has a limited supply of water to dive in. Finding work is a constant challenge.

Learner diver

Having completed the diving lessons, the learner diver must pass a practical diving test followed by a series of theoretical diving questions.

"Good. Now just a few questions on the Offshore Code."

"Quite frankly, I joined the diving branch to get away from all of this."

Military diver

Shrouded in secrecy and equipped with state-of-the-art technology, there is no sea too rough nor job too tough for the intrepid military diver. Due to the unusually rigorous conditions in which these divers have to work, the normal level of military discipline tends to be more relaxed than usual.

Old diver

Young divers are becoming a rare collectable. Tax incentives may have to be offered for cornering one. Senior divers will probably need their IMCA hearing aids, glasses, replacement hips and pace-makers to stand a chance.

"Where have all the young divers gone?"

Pearl diver

A specialist type of treasure diver, the pearl diver risks his life on a daily basis in the hope that one day he will find that priceless pearl and never need to work again. This, of course, is a chance in a million but if he succeeds, the world is his oyster.

PLA diver

The Port of London Authority diver cannot survive more than a few miles out of London. These divers work routinely in the river Thames – usually in zero visibility and often in polluted water. Such stressful conditions can lead to hallucinations in susceptible individuals.

"Poor chap ... he keeps insisting he saw a fish."

"Get ready. Here comes another one!"

Police diver

While recreational divers frolic amongst the underwater flora and fauna, and commercial divers are earning a crust, the police diver has much more serious matters to contend with.

Receiver of Wreck

Though not a type of diver, the Receiver of Wreck is a familiar adjudicator in salvage operations ensuring fair play both for salvors and owners of wrecked property. The first Receiver was appointed some 150 years ago establishing a *menage à trois* with the salvor and owner.

This happy threesome has more recently been joined by the HSE: the owner keeps an eye on the salvor, who keeps an eye on the Receiver, who keeps an eye on the wreck. The HSE keeps an eye on them all.

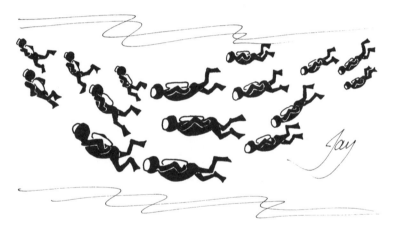

School of divers

Schooling is a natural phenomenon in diving. Scientists believe it is a defensive behavioural tactic exhibited in the presence of predatory tax divers. The solitary diver is particularly vulnerable and, if caught unawares, should immediately seek a shoal of accountant divers.

Scientific diver

The most outstanding distinguishing features of the scientific diver are his insatiable curiosity and relentless determination to scrutinise the object of his attention at an unnaturally close range. This means he sometimes misses the bigger picture which frequently exposes him to risk of physical injury.

"You'd never get me up in one of those things."

Scuba diver

After centuries of breath-hold diving, this cheeky little diver exploded on the scene in the mid 20th century. Scuba divers reproduce at an alarming rate and are now the most common form of diver on earth. Vast shoals of scuba divers can be found in holiday resorts around the world. The freedom from having to remain on the ocean floor enables the scuba diver to perform eye-popping mid-water aquabatics that makes it, frankly, an impertinent show-off. Not all divers can make the transition.

Skin diver

Skin divers are minimalists when it comes to diving equipment ... in fact, they might be mistaken for skint divers.

In order to avoid giving offence to less liberated divers, they tend to inhabit remote sites. For obvious reasons, they shrink away from cold water areas.

Sky diver

The sky diver is not yet included in the HSE qualification system due to teething problems with the practical test. Sky divers imagine they are a cut above the rest. Regulations, however, will inevitably bring them down to earth.

Standby diver

Regulations require that all diving operations are carried out with a standby diver in attendance. The long-life standby diver is a handy accessory in any diving team. Regular testing is required to ensure that the standby diver does not exceed his shelf life.

Student diver

The student diver must be able to withstand intensive and protracted training. Occasionally one may crack under the pressure.

Trainee bell diver

The trainee bell diver is one of the most adaptable of divers. Initially an 'HSE Part II diver,' the trainee bell diver has had to adapt to being called a 'bell diver,' a 'saturation diver' and finally an 'HSE closed bell diver' without moving a muscle. Confused trainee bell divers can determine their current classification by referring to the HSE *Diving at Work Regulations 1997 List of Approved Diving Qualifications.*

".. and this is the button for extra sugar."

"And finally, what work do you have lined up for next year?"

Unemployed diver

It is well known that ROVs have displaced many divers from their traditional roles. Trade associations are most concerned and carry out relentless surveys.

DIVING TASKS

There is no limit to the range of tasks a diver may be called upon to perform. The mind boggles.
For the afflicted, hyperbaric boggling is covered in the section on Diving Medicine.

"This is your first time with bolt stretchers, right?"

Bolt tensioning

One of the most useful tools available to divers who work on pipe flanges is the hydraulic bolt stretcher. Though simple in concept, the many components can appear at first glance to be a bit complicated. But with patience and practice, the installation and operation of a bolt stretcher can be easily mastered.

Buoyancy bags

Buoyancy bags don't all have to look the same. With a little imagination and practice they can be transformed into works of art.

"Ivor just can't help himself. He used to be a children's entertainer."

Butt welding

This is a common type of welding and, as with all welding procedures, it is extremely important to first get into a comfortable position. The recommended position is illustrated. Individual welders may have alternative preferences.

Cable burial

All sorts of cables and flexible lines need to be buried under the sea bed for their own protection. Normally special sleds or ploughs are used but occasionally divers have to be called in to assist.

"I'll be glad when they've repaired the f***ing cable plough."

Drilling support

Oilfield diving is particularly hazardous because of the possibility of an accidental blow-out. Oil companies spend a fortune developing blow-out preventers to reduce this risk. Oilfield divers are required to familiarise themselves with these protective safety devices.

High pressure water jetting

This is an effective method of removing hard concretions from steel structures. The pressure of the water delivery must be carefully controlled to achieve maximum efficiency.

"Just a shade less pressure, surface."

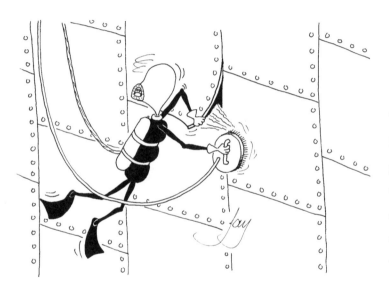

Hull cleaning

The invaluable work done by the hull-cleaning diver helps ships maintain good cruising speeds and high fuel economy. Comprehensive quality control measures are necessary to ensure that no 'short-cuts' have been taken.

Hyperbaric welding

Hyperbaric welding requires the ability to maintain a high level of un-interrupted concentration even in the face of annoying distractions.

"I've told you a hundred times. Don't call me at work."

"Let's see . . . I think I'll go for a number three iron on this one."

Magnetic particle inspection (MPI)

This is one of the most important tasks carried out by inspection divers. Using a combination of magnetism and fluorescent ink, tiny cracks in steel structures can be visualised. Paradoxically, a good handicap can be an advantage.

Metrology

One of the most important tasks for the offshore construction diver is the taking of accurate measurements for the fabrication of pipeline spool pieces. This is a critical skill that can only be acquired through constant practice.

"Wow! Did you see that tide go out!"

Pipe flanging

Pipe flanging is a standard task for divers. Care is required when working in poor visibility, strong currents and particularly in areas where there are big tides.

Torque wrenching

This clever tool allows the diver to tighten even the largest nuts with the minimum of effort. The tool does all the work and all the diver has to do is to install it carefully. The tool takes all the pressure off the diver and helps him to unwind.

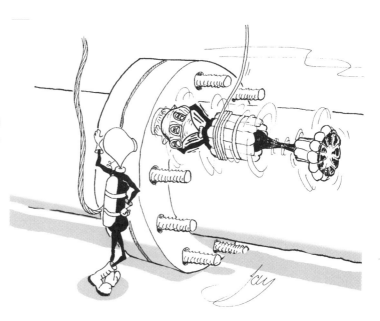

"Dammit ... It says here, 'batteries not included'."

Ultrasonic NDT

Whilst instruments get smaller and smaller, manuals get bigger and bigger. It is usually a good idea to read the manuals cover-to-cover before using the instrument at the work site.

Underwater concreting

There is a knack to pouring concrete underwater. The end of the tremie tube must remain immersed in the concrete during the pour. The diver, on the other hand, shouldn't ... especially when using a quick-setting variety.

"And then I said, 'Make it hot' . . . "

Underwater cutting

Oxy-arc cutting is very effective under water. However, only well-trained divers should attempt it. Unskilled divers may find it shockingly hazardous to their health.

Use of explosives

The effectiveness of an explosive charge can be increased by expert shaping. This can also reduce the size of the charge required. This skill has now reached the status of an art-form.

"You have to admit, when it comes to shaped charges, Ivor's a real artist."

Wreck salvage

Wreck salvage is a significant market for specialist underwater contractors. However, before work can commence, and in the interest of safety at sea, it is important that any hazard to navigation is reliably marked.

PLANT AND EQUIPMENT

Every time I see a sign at the side of the road stating
"Heavy plant crossing" I expect to see a Triffid
dragging itself across the road in front of me. I am
severely afflicted with 'literalism'.
Diving equipment offers a rich vein of inspiration.
Just the mention of bells, pigs and umbilicals plays
havoc with my imagination.

"Sorry Ivor, but you HAVE to come out.
This is the washing machine."

The Deck Compression Chamber (DCC)

DCCs come in a variety of colours and can be assembled in an almost infinite variety of configurations to suit the customer. Lego enthusiasts love them. Under normal operating conditions they deliver excellent performance – a full weekly load of saturated divers tumble out dry, fresh and squeaky clean.

Diamond wire cutter

The unique hardness of precious diamonds is exploited in this high-tech tool. Nothing can resist its cutting edge technology. The tool has become so popular that special precautions are needed to protect it.

Diver umbilical

Some divers are not made; they are simply born to be divers ... especially naval divers.

Diving bell

A diver's street-cred can rely on his image. He must have all the latest gadgets and accessories. Bell-upmanship is permitted, if tastefully done.

"Wow! Did you say it has air conditioning AND heave compensation fitted as standard?"

Diving ladder

In the age of high-tech diving, it is good to know that one of the oldest and most reliable pieces of diving equipment is still in regular use – the diving ladder. However, it would be a mistake to rely on it in isolation.

Diving tank

Familiar to all trainee divers is the diving tank. It brings back fond memories of their first big splash into diving. But there are splashes and splashes. Inevitably, some splashes are bigger than others.

"No, son. The diving tank is over here".

"Oh ... THAT's the hot water unit."

Hot water unit

While divers like to be cool, they do not appreciate being given a cold shoulder. There is a limit to how much they will tolerate, especially at depth.
Deep is cool; deep frozen is un-cool.

Hyperbaric lifeboat

In the event of an imminent catastrophe, divers should assemble at their nearest hyperbaric lifeboat station in an orderly and controlled manner. Any tendency to panic must be avoided.

"I said we should have left it where we could see it."

Missing equipment

Some dive neighbourhoods are dodgier than others. In suspect locations, long excursions are not recommended.

Oxygen reducer

Some parts of a diving system are highly dangerous and need to be handled with great care. The oxygen reducer is one such component. All it takes is one bright spark to set it off. It is a complex piece of machinery. Exploded views can help to identify its various parts. In the case of very small ones, these can be blown up.

Oxygen reducer, exploded view.

"I'm all for ships of opportunity. The trouble with this one is the penalty clause states: 'two dozen lashes at the gangway'."

Ship of opportunity

In these competitive times, one way to reduce overheads is to use ships of opportunity. However, terms and conditions vary from ship to ship. Care should be taken to read the small print.

Swiss diving bell

Diving equipment manufacturing is a competitive international business. Many companies vie for prominence, constantly bringing out newer models and accessories in the race to keep ahead. The Swiss have made particular advances in this area.

"It's life Jymnn, but not as we know it."

Transponder

Where on earth would divers be without transponders? These ubiquitous devices are on constant duty helping divers, ROVs and vessels work out exactly where they are and where they are going. They may be the most intelligent form of life on the seabed. Divers would be all at sea without them.

DIVING TECHNIQUES

For every type of diver, in every type of task, there is
an optimum technique. Fortunately, there is a wide
range of optimum techniques available.

Assisted ascent

In emergency, when all else fails, the last resort of the diver is to return to the surface as quickly as possible. Assisted ascent is fast and efficient and recommended for all situations when it's time to go ballistic.

Bell cross-hauling

When a diving bell has to be placed in a tight spot, it is sometimes necessary to cross-haul the bell. A variety of arrangements can be used to swing the bell away from under the main lift winch. In complicated situations, the bell hoisting position may be transferred several times. On these occasions, clear directions are imperative.

"Swing a left at the christmas tree; throw a right at the manifold and take the third flowline to the jacket. You can't miss it".

Bell diving

Bell divers need a lot of patience when commuting to and from work. Unfortunately, they have to rely on others to keep to the schedule. But Supervisors are only human too!

"Typical. You wait ages and then three come along together."

Bell lock-out diving

Time passes quickly when you're enjoying yourself. Over-enthusiastic divers must be careful not to over-stay their welcome. Sea organisms may be fascinating, but they can grow on you.

"Now that was one long lock-out."

Booted diving

A diver working on the sea-bed often prefers to work in heavy work boots rather than fins. There is a subtle distinction between finned and booted divers. The illustration should help clarify the difference.

Decompression stops

When a diver returns to the surface he must do so in a controlled manner. Depending on the depth and duration of the dive, the diver may have to stop his ascent in stages to avoid getting the bends. These stops can be very protracted and boring. Sympathetic supervisors do their best to make them more interesting.

"Deco-stops were never like this when I started diving".

"Ivor likes to dive heavy."

Diving heavy

Divers sometimes become entrenched in the habit of wearing extra weight when working in strong currents. The more extreme cases plough a lonely furrow.

Hell diving

Hell diving is closely related to bell diving. It is diabolical. It happens when every damn thing goes wrong and it becomes a devil of a job.

"No water? No water!
What sort of place do you call this?"

Oilfield diving

Diving techniques have to be constantly modified to meet the fast-changing technology in the oil industry. Unfortunately, some of the changes eliminate the need for divers.

"I hear the latest oil wells are completely diver-less."

Polluted water diving

You wouldn't believe what some divers have to dive in. Diving in polluted water can cause serious illnesses. Signs and symptoms include feeling flushed and going round the bend.

"Well done Ivor.
27 minutes — a personal best".

Wet welding

After a slow start, wet welding has finally arrived. Experienced contractors should have no difficulty in telling the difference between a wet and dry welder. For everyone else, the accompanying illustration may help.

DIVING MEDICINE AND SAFETY

This section is not for the squeamish. Skip it if you faint at the sight of blood or pimples. However, if you aspire to the dizzy height of a Diving Medic, then I'm afraid this section is obligatory reading. An honours degree in Latin might help.

Codes of Practice

Some aspects of diving can be hazardous. To help divers cope, the government helpfully issues more and more rules.
Happy reading!

Dehydration

Water figures prominently in a diver's life. Lots of it – both inside and out is highly recommended for maximum diving performance.

"Water ... water ..."

Diving doctor

Every diver needs a diving doctor ... or, more accurately, a diving medical. Fortunately, diving doctors are ready to spring into action at a moment's notice.

External ear infection

Divers often complain of ear infections. A wide range of fungi and other exotic flora and fauna are always lurking about, looking for an opportunity to set up home in a warm, damp diver's ear. They can lead to deafness. So keep taking the ear-drops. I said, 'KEEP TAKING THE EAR-DROPS!'

"We haven't been taking our ear-drops, have we?"

"Dr Mumbo claims he has a cure for the bends and
has brought along one of his patients to show you"
[IMCA recognises Diver Medics]

IMCA diver medics

IMCA has established a healthy standard in recognising the qualification of the diver medic. This should eliminate the great variation in international standards.

Limb bend

Even a careful diver can have the misfortune to suffer a limb bend. Keeping up the pressure is the only solution.

"I see you're still getting treament for the leg."

Spatial awareness

Occasionally divers can become disorientated. Any diver who feels he is on the brink of flipping, should seek urgent medical advice.

"Sad really. They're completely helpless until someone turns them back over?"

Risk assessment 1

Every job is fraught with potential hazards. So now no job can proceed without a risk assessment. Traditionally dangerous jobs are made safer this way. Britain and Norway have reciprocal rules governing risk assessments.

"We can still plunder and pillage but now we have to prepare a risk assessment first"

"That is the worst case of Risk Assessment
Fatigue I have ever seen"

Risk assessment 2

Producing a Risk Assessment can be a
demanding, even exhausting, exercise.
It should not be attempted without prior
training and preparation. Divers should
carefully evaluate the associated risks before
embarking on such a hazardous exercise.

Underwater life forms

Every diver should to be able to identify the marine
flora and fauna around him. This is not only to assist
in the inspection duty to his client but also to protect
himself from potential hazards. Risk assessments
should refer to any likely close encounters.

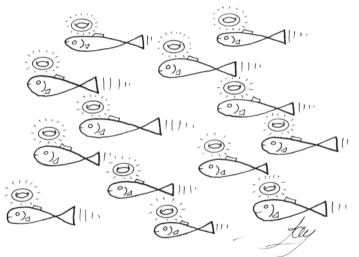

Angel fish

The heavenly angel fish (the underwater equivalent of the bird of paradise) is a familiar sight to warm water divers. The illustration depicts a band of exotic juveniles. Adults grow wings and can occasionally be seen flitting above the waves in tropical climes.

Artificial reef

Scientists are keen to encourage thriving populations of sea life. To this end they are designing habitat-friendly artificial reefs.

"You'll love it here. Tasty new neighbours move in downstairs every day"

"Didn't you see that banana fish?"

Banana fish

The bottom-living banana fish is a master of deception. It lurks around disguised as an accident waiting to happen.
It is frequently blamed for many an underwater slip-up.

Bottlenose dolphin and Hammerhead shark

In the interests of safety, divers are advised never to intervene in violent underwater disputes.

(For those who may be interested, in this instance the dolphin got hammered and bottled out).

"Who are you calling 'Bottlenose', Hammerhead?"

"Hey, Ivor ... did you see that clown fish?"

Clown fish

Ever the comedian, the clown fish can seriously distract a diver from his work. Divers should avoid them at all costs. A diver wouldn't wish one on his worst anemone.

Dogfish

Some days are just plain sh***y. Watch where you step and blame it on the dog fish.

"Ugh! Darn dogfish!"

Elephant fish

The diver must always be prepared to encounter the unexpected underwater. The elusive elephant fish is a prime example. To date, the legendary Elephant Fish Graveyard, the final resting place of these magnificent creatures, remains a mystery.

Hound fish

Not all underwater leaks can be easily resolved. Expert inspection by the appropriate authorities can usually identify the cause. However, the alleged existence of a monster hound fish has yet to be scientifically proven.

"Just as I suspected. This is the work of the dastardly houndfish."

"Ignore them ... it's just a cry for attention."

Jellyfish

Divers must always be alert to the danger of stinging jellyfish. These can be accidentally sucked into the seawater intakes for hot-water suits and their stinging cells distributed inside the suit. Fortunately not all jellyfish are vicious. They come in all sorts of shapes, sizes and flavours ranging from the plain to the exotic. This can lead to friction between some species.

Martians

The ocean is a vast and mostly unexplored domain. Divers may occasionally encounter new, unidentified forms of life (usually referred to a 'Type 3 close encounter'). Divers should record sightings in the "What the hell was that?" section of their logbooks.

"Don't look Zcerikz. It's horrible .... horrible."

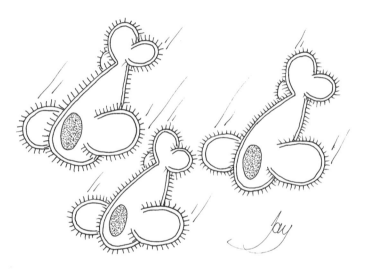

Phyterplankton

Recent research has revealed an aggressive new species of plankton in the northern Atlantic. Deadly killers, these ferocious little creatures swoop in 'squadrons' and can devour an entire protozoa in seconds.

Piranha fish

Divers in South America need to know
how to identify piranhas, preferably before
the piranhas indentify them.

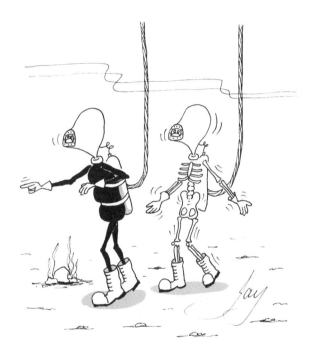

"Now, if I am not mistaken, that was a shoal of
piranha fish."

"And whatever you do, don't touch that!
It's a protected species."

Protected species

Conservationists have extraordinary powers to prevent any injury occurring to protected marine species. To qualify for this special treatment all you need to be is an endangered creature. So why shouldn't divers be a protected species too?

Sea snake

This dangerous marine animal must be treated with care. While the diving suit normally offers effective protection from its venomous bite, its appetite should not be underestimated. Sea snakes like divers – but they can probably eat only one at a time. Dive with a buddy.

"Hang on, Ivor. I've spotted a sea snake track."

"It's life Jim, but not as we know it."

Volcanic vent worms

These deceptively intelligent life-forms have evolved around deep ocean hot-water vents. They have achieved the ultimate in living a life of complete luxury.

ROVs AND AUVs

These vehicles are underwater acronyms. An acronym is not a female acrobat. An acronym is word (AAIAW) made up of (MUO) the initial letters of a series of words (TILOASOWs). This is to make things simpler. It would have been easier, for example, if I had simply written AAAMUOTILOASOWs). Right?

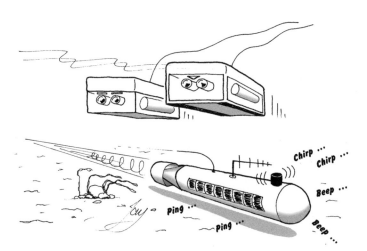

"Noisy brat! It's not even on a lead."

The AUV

Well-controlled ROVs must think AUVs are insolent pups that need to attend obedience classes. Their antics are enough to drive their owners barking mad.

AUV commensalism

The role of the AUV in the ever-evolving subsea ecosystem is illustrated in this example of a commensal, symbiotic relationship.

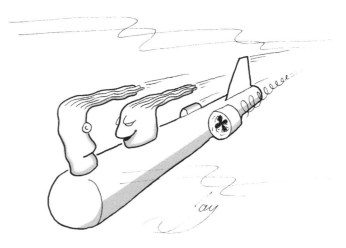

"Once you've tried one of these, you'll never look at another hermit crab again."

"Sorry my sweet, the batteries are flat."

AUV power sources

The longevity of the power source of an AUV is a critical factor in its successful operation.

AUV recharging

One of the most important factors in AUV operations is the arrangement for recharging the batteries ... which can now be done underwater without having to recover the AUV.

AUV way point

A way point is a geographical location used by AUVs as a reference point, generally where a change in direction is planned. Any one mssion may have several way points. The more way points, the more challenging the task.

AUV world record

Hardly a day goes by without another world record being broken by an AUV. The technology is racing ahead so fast that it is getting difficult to keep up with it all.

"I suppose that means it's broken another world record."

"It's ridiculous. Only last week it was the gas and electricity."

Cable burial plough

Cable burial is an essential aspect of the long-term integrity of subsea cables. So many criss-cross the ocean floor that it seems that no sooner is one trench filled than it is dug up again for yet another cable.

Eyeball ROV

A great step forward in diver safety is the introduction of the eyeball ROV, hovering over the diver's shoulder watching his every move. Not all divers find this particularly comforting. Perhaps the illustration will reassure them.

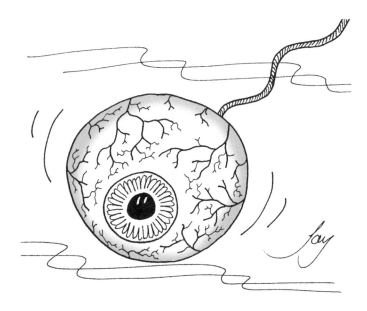

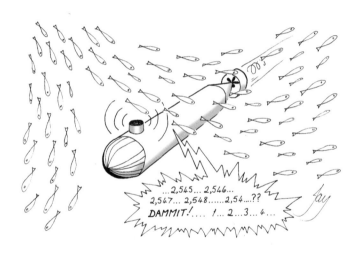

Fish-counting AUV

One of the amazing tasks carried out by AUVs is fish-counting. The trouble starts when one of the counters hiccups.

Government surplus AUV

AUVs are inherently very expensive beasts. So it is understandable that scientific bodies try to economise. Sometimes this can turn out to be a false economy.

"We sometimes get this trouble with the AUVs that we build from government-surplus torpedo bodies."

IMCA ROV

The International Marine Contractors Association represents the major offshore diving and underwater construction companies, not to mention the DP vessel operators. Committees representing diving, remote systems and ROVs are particularly pro-active.

Inspection AUV

First divers did the inspection. Then ROVs took over the job from divers. Now AUVs are taking over the job from ROVs. Who's next?

"Remember when we used to do that."

"Oh no. Not another stray."

Lost AUV

A major disadvantage of the AUV is its ability to lose its bearings and get lost. Fortunately, a major advantage of ROVs is their ability to rescue lost AUVs.

ROV accident

As the undersea gets busier and more crowded, inevitably there is going to be the occasional collision between ROVs. These can be largely avoided with the careful use of obstacle avoidance sonar.

"Move along please ... there's nothing to see."

ROV breakdown I

Although the mean-time-between-failures of ROVs is improving all the time, there are still enough ROV breakdowns to provide work opportunities for divers.

ROV breakdown 2

The ROV maintenance technician must be prepared for the most unlikely failure modes. This is why good training is so essential.

"It's dampness I'm afraid."

"Sorry Sir, but you'll have to queue with the rest of them."

ROV exhibition

AUVs and ROVs are getting so popular these days that they even have their own exhibitions and conferences. To avoid disappointment, it is always recommended to register in advance.

ROV garage

Work-class ROVs are sometimes deployed from a garage. A tether management system is included with the garage to pay out and recover the ROV tether. Great skill is required in manoeuvring the ROV back into the garage – it is a tight fit. This has to be carried out very carefully and slowly to avoid damage.

"... and watch out for those flying ROVs."

ROV hazard

Divers and ROV pilots must exercise great care when working in close proximity with each other. Divers in particular must keep a keen eye out for potential ROV hazards.

ROV maintenance

ROV systems require a strict maintenance regime of perodic inspection and testing. This should include rigorous exercising of all manipulator functions.

"Forty two, ... forty three, ... forty ... four..."

"Poor thing. He's at the end of his tether."

ROV tether

A major advantage of the AUV over the ROV is the freedom from a restraining tether. Tether-stress is a common cause of ROV breakdowns. Sympathetic fault analysis treatment can help in some cases.

Wild AUVs

There is nothing more magnificent than the sight of a shoal of wild AUVs in mid-ocean, just as nature intended.

"Isn't it awesome when you see them in the wild."

Work class ROV

The work class ROV is the work-horse of the ROV world. It is tough and strong and is not afraid of getting its manipulators dirty. The work class ROV looks up to the middle class ROV which, in turn, looks up to the upper class ROV.